SHARK

BRIAN SKERRY

NATIONAL
GEOGRAPHIC

WASHINGTON, D.C.

CONTENTS

FIRST PAGE: A tiger shark swims over a coral reef in the Bahamas, with a nurse shark (left) and a Caribbean reef shark (right) in the background.

PREVIOUS PAGES: Whale sharks are the largest fish that currently exist.

LEFT: A blacktip reef shark patrols the reef at Millennium Atoll, a tropical paradise that has been largely unmarred by human activity.

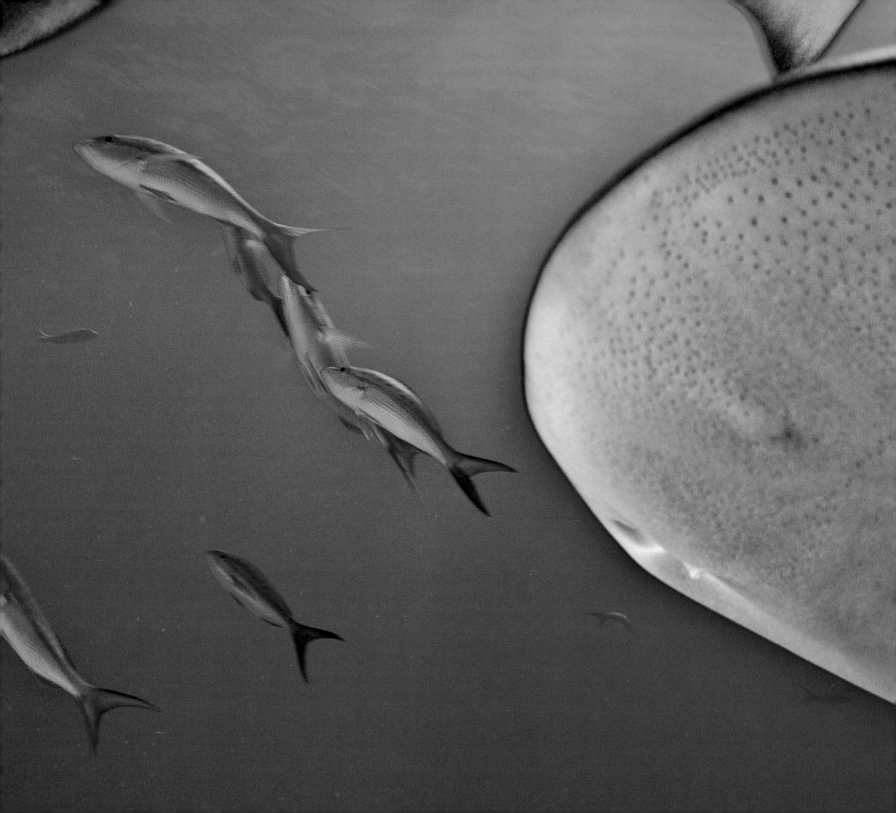

PREVIOUS PAGES: A Caribbean reef shark investigates the camera in the Bahamas.

Scientists have found that ecosystems with strong reefs are often home to large populations of top predators such as whitetip reef sharks (foreground) and gray reef sharks (background). A thriving reef can support plenty of smaller marine life, allowing these predators to coexist peacefully.

Oceanic whitetips are elusive creatures, and Cat Island in the Bahamas is home to one of their last known strongholds. As recently as the 1970s, they were one of the most abundant large animals on the planet, but their numbers have since dwindled to about one percent of their historic population.

INTRODUCTION

overall supremacy in the sea, I have also come to see sharks as a fragile species, vulnerable to the hand of humans. As a journalist, I am driven by a sense of responsibility and a sense of urgency to broadcast what I have learned: that sharks are integral to the planet's health and that they are in trouble and need our help. There are more than 400 species of sharks swimming Earth's oceans, yet only a few get attention. And the notoriety received is mostly negative and frequently associated with a public threat. Although in recent years much has been done to better educate the public and to dispel the one-dimensional view of sharks as mindless monsters, I believe the makeover of sharks must continue in earnest. They must be portrayed with

to specific locations based on what they've learned. Tracking the movements of sand tigers using tags is revealing that sharks may also have more complex social structures than we recognize, not unlike those of marine mammals such as dolphins. With new information about sharks emerging every year, I wonder, What will we learn tomorrow? I think about the wisdom this ancient species possesses and muse about the potential to learn from them.

To the degree that I can do so through still images, my hope is to convey the personality of sharks. The notion of animal personality is something once scoffed at by science, yet today researchers are openly discussing such concepts. Any pet owner can attest to the fact that animals demonstrate unique

I AM DRIVEN BY A SENSE OF RESPONSIBILITY AND A SENSE OF URGENCY TO BROADCAST WHAT I HAVE LEARNED: THAT SHARKS ARE INTEGRAL TO THE PLANET'S HEALTH AND THAT THEY ARE IN TROUBLE AND NEED OUR HELP.

more attention to their nuances and greater awareness of their importance to the natural balance of the environment.

When an animal is seen as dangerous or bad, eliminating it invites little objection. And so it has been for sharks, with more than 100 million killed annually, largely for their fins, which become the prime ingredient in a popular soup. While we are far from fully understanding shark behaviors, science is revealing a more complex view of these animals. We are learning that species such as white sharks may live well past age 70 and that their annual migrations and life cycles are more complicated and far less predictable than other fish. Evidence also suggests that they are capable of creating new feeding strategies to capitalize on prey in specific locations. Researchers believe that tiger sharks might develop annual feeding patterns based on discovery—that they may have the cognitive ability to remember and return

personalities, and I believe this to be true with wild animals, too. Caribbean reef sharks exhibit personality traits different from those of mako sharks, and individual animals within a given species have their own character and temperament as well. If we can alter our view of sharks and begin to see them as magnificent and as having value, the existing dynamic can change.

This book offers a glimpse into the world of these apex ocean predators. Far from completely understood and still somewhat enigmatic, they demand that we see them as they are, not as we imagine them to be. Not huggable domesticated pets, but also not demons whose eradication is acceptable. Each species is unique, possessing biology and abilities perfectly suited to reign supreme within the habitat in which they live. As we see sharks in a new light, perhaps appreciation will follow and, with that, a desire to celebrate and conserve. ■

My first encounter with a blue shark helped shape my fascination and affection for sharks.

1 Great white shark VU
Carcharodon carcharias
This legendary predator lives in coastal surface waters worldwide.

Anal fin

Length: 15-20 ft

Actual size of tooth

Serrations may be a link to extinct ancestors.

View from below

4 Tiger shark NT
Galeocerdo cuvier
This shark is named for its distinct black stripes, which fade in adulthood.

14-18 ft

Status

VU Vulnerable

EN Endangered

NT Near threatened

CR Critically endangered

ID Insufficient data

Diet

Sea turtles

Seals, sea lions

Fish

Sea birds

Crustaceans, mollusks

Sharks, rays

Cetaceans

Plankton

2 Great hammerhead shark EN
Sphyrna mokarran
A wide head helps these sharks scan for and pin down rays and other prey.

15-20 ft

5 Greenland shark NT
Somniosus microcephalus
Scientists suspect that this slow-growing Arctic species can live up to a hundred years.

16-21 ft

3 Whale shark VU
Rhincodon typus
This slow-moving, filter-feeding shark is the largest known fish species alive.

SHARKS
LORDS OF THE SEA

There are more than 500 species of sharks, predators crucial to maintaining ecosystem balance. Scientists estimate that more than 70 species are threatened with extinction, mostly because of overfishing.

● ANGEL SHARKS   SAWSHARKS   ● DOGFISH SHARKS

Long snout   Short snout

Ray-like body   Not ray-like

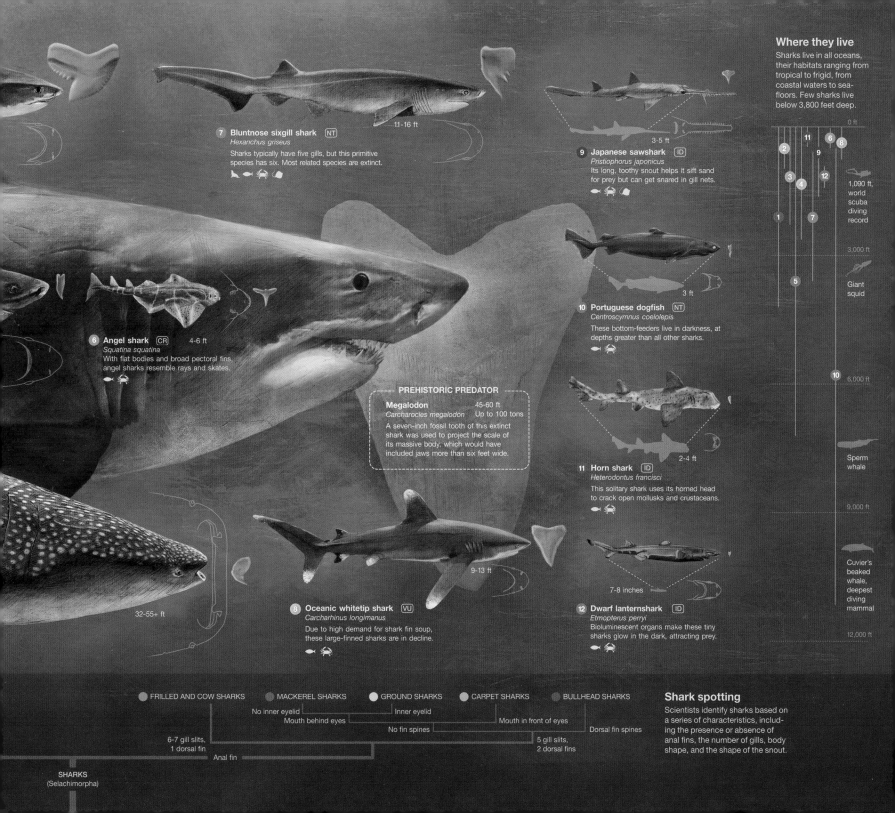

7 Bluntnose sixgill shark NT
Hexanchus griseus
Sharks typically have five gills, but this primitive species has six. Most related species are extinct.

11-16 ft

9 Japanese sawshark ID
Pristiophorus japonicus
Its long, toothy snout helps it sift sand for prey but can get snared in gill nets.

3-5 ft

6 Angel shark CR   4-6 ft
Squatina squatina
With flat bodies and broad pectoral fins, angel sharks resemble rays and skates.

10 Portuguese dogfish NT
Centroscymnus coelolepis
These bottom-feeders live in darkness, at depths greater than all other sharks.

PREHISTORIC PREDATOR

Megalodon   45-60 ft
Carcharocles megalodon   Up to 100 tons
A seven-inch fossil tooth of this extinct shark was used to project the scale of its massive body, which would have included jaws more than six feet wide.

3 ft

11 Horn shark ID
Heterodontus francisci
This solitary shark uses its horned head to crack open mollusks and crustaceans.

2-4 ft

8 Oceanic whitetip shark VU
Carcharhinus longimanus
Due to high demand for shark fin soup, these large-finned sharks are in decline.

9-13 ft

32-55+ ft

7-8 inches

12 Dwarf lanternshark ID
Etmopterus perryi
Bioluminescent organs make these tiny sharks glow in the dark, attracting prey.

Where they live
Sharks live in all oceans, their habitats ranging from tropical to frigid, from coastal waters to sea-floors. Few sharks live below 3,800 feet deep.

0 ft

1,090 ft, world scuba diving record

3,000 ft

Giant squid

6,000 ft

Sperm whale

9,000 ft

Cuvier's beaked whale, deepest diving mammal

12,000 ft

FRILLED AND COW SHARKS   MACKEREL SHARKS   GROUND SHARKS   CARPET SHARKS   BULLHEAD SHARKS

No inner eyelid   Inner eyelid
Mouth behind eyes   Mouth in front of eyes
No fin spines   Dorsal fin spines
6-7 gill slits,   5 gill slits,
1 dorsal fin   2 dorsal fins
Anal fin

SHARKS
(Selachimorpha)

Shark spotting
Scientists identify sharks based on a series of characteristics, including the presence or absence of anal fins, the number of gills, body shape, and the shape of the snout.

CHAPTER ONE

FLUID PERFECTION

SHARKS—THE EPITOME OF EVOLUTIONARY EXCELLENCE

The challenge of photographing sharks: to show how six million years of evolution results in species perfectly adapted to their habitats.

BRIAN SKERRY

It was humid and hot—at least 95°F—and the mosquitoes were thick. As I bushwhacked my way through a dense mangrove channel, sweat burned my eyes and bugs covered my hands. The water was knee-deep in places, and, holding my camera at chest level to keep it dry, I slogged on until reaching a clearing. I was standing in a very shallow natural pool of seawater, surrounded by mangrove trees and hidden from the world. I was also standing in the middle of a nursery for baby sharks.

Standing with me in this tranquil setting on the Bahamian island of Bimini was Samuel "Doc" Gruber, a legendary shark scientist and the founder of the Bimini Sharklab. Doc had discovered this site and took me to it so that I might find and photograph lemon shark pups. Mangroves sink their roots down underwater, creating a dense network of trees along shallow coastal regions, and that becomes a natural nursery for juvenile ocean animals, because larger predators cannot penetrate the undergrowth to reach them. Lemon sharks typically have their pups in early June, and the young sharks spend the first couple of years of their lives within the mangroves.

I had come here in hopes of seeing this very scene and to make pictures that would present a view of sharks not often witnessed. The fact is, it is not especially difficult to make scary images of sharks, and although some of my images might fall into this category, most often I resist the temptation, for I do not wish to perpetuate the notion of sharks as monsters. Photographs of baby sharks, I thought, might show them as multidimensional creatures with

---

PREVIOUS PAGES: A silvertip shark glides effortlessly through the water off the east coast of South Africa.

their own vulnerabilities—and might thereby help convey a more complete picture of the ocean, where every animal and every habitat plays a role.

To produce pictures of these little lemons within their nurseries, I needed to be underwater. But here the water was only about a foot deep. So wearing only a wet suit, mask, and snorkel, I had to lie flat in the mangrove. Leaving the hot, sunny, buggy surface world for a time, I slid my head underwater. I felt like Alice falling through the looking glass, for instantly I was swept away to another realm. It was a world of seagrass and sand, of mangrove roots and baby fish such as snapper. The palette was largely monochromatic, a pale green, liquid universe, and the water was filled with fine particles of silt. I spent most of the day lying in the mangrove, with only fleeting glimpses of the sharks at the edge of my visibility. As I returned day after day, it seemed as though the pups were becoming acclimated to me, swimming a bit closer and checking me out. It was a surreal experience, being literally in two worlds at the same time: my back exposed to the sunny air-breathing world, my face and brain entranced in a place where foot-long sharks swam confidently among mangrove roots in shallow water.

MY CUSTOMARY APPROACH to underwater photography assignments is to observe and show the interactions between creatures and their habitats. I focus first on specific parts of an ecosystem, then eventually step back and see the big picture. Some of the most interesting natural history images are those that show an animal within its habitat. There is often something peaceful and serene about such renderings, and I find them especially insightful because they offer context and help us understand how things fit together in the larger natural world. Images such as this are harder to make underwater. First of all, only in the clearest of waters is this possible. Sometimes the habitat of a shark is simply the open ocean, and therefore a picture in blue water accurately portrays the animal's home. But whenever possible I seek to show a portion of the benthic region—the ocean floor, the lowest region underwater—for it leads us into the shark's realm in a special way.

During a dive in the temperate waters of New Zealand's Fiordland, for example, I was photographing tiny animals on the fiord wall using a macro lens. I happened to look up at the right time and saw in the distance a shark swimming toward me. My assistant was carrying my wide-angle camera

WHAT ALWAYS STRIKES ME FIRST IS THE SYMMETRY,
THE FLAWLESS BALANCE THAT SHARKS DISPLAY.
EACH SPECIES HAS EVOLVED TO EXCEL WITHIN ITS HABITAT.

They were perfect, miniature copies of adult lemon sharks. Sometimes they would race through the mangrove, while other times they gracefully navigated their way around the roots and leaves. In this rather controlled setting I was able to fully observe these little predators and see just how perfectly they had been sculpted by nature. They ascended, descended, and banked like a fighter jet and were able to turn on a dime. If I made even a slight disruption to the mirror-calm surface, they knew it instantly, their body's lateral line tuned to receive the slightest of vibrations telegraphed through the water. It was abundantly clear that even here, within a nursery for juvenile marine animals, the little sharks were in charge.

system, so I swapped rigs and swam toward the shark, which I eventually recognized as a sevengill. The water was green and light levels were low, even on a sunny day. It was like swimming through a dimly lit cathedral. The visibility was not great, but with the wide-angle lens I was able to make a frame that showed the shark in a larger setting that defined its world. The steep, rocky fiord walls were covered with life. Small fish darted in and out, and invertebrates carpeted the walls: sponges, tunicates, and sea stars that created a tapestry of muted colors, a blend of yellows, rusty oranges, and reds.

If I am in a place where I can see sharks often, my photo coverage can progress from the entire animal to individual parts of the animal to the shark within its landscape—but it always starts with the shark itself. These animals demand my focus. At the first sight of a shark on any dive, I am immediately drawn to the animal and want to make pictures that capture it fully. If I have repeated opportunities, I will shoot from multiple angles, trying to squeeze the shutter at the moment when the animal's gesture and grace define its essence. I want to produce an image that exudes the shark's life force and

fins, like the wings of a glider, allowing them to cruise over lengthy distances without wasting energy. Pelagic zones have been described as ocean deserts with sporadic pockets of life. To thrive in such a landscape, these sharks must be especially efficient. I can imagine a blue shark or whitetip gliding downward, half a mile deep into the sea, expending barely any energy in search of its next meal. The hydrodynamic shape slices through

I MARVEL AT ALL MARINE CREATURES AND WISH I POSSESSED THE ABILITY TO MOVE EFFORTLESSLY, AS THEY DO, THROUGH THE SEA. BUT I AM MOST HUMBLED AND MOST IN AWE OF THE SHARK.

personality. If even more chances are afforded, I slow down a bit and begin to observe the individual parts of a shark's exquisite anatomy. I honestly believe that if given the chance, I could be content to spend a month just making pictures of dorsal fins. I am equally fascinated by shark tails and can imagine a future photo exhibit whose theme celebrates only these impressive anatomical features.

MORE OFTEN THAN NOT, whenever I head off on assignment I am traveling to a place I have never been before. My initial dives are usually spent mostly looking around and watching, trying to make sense of all that I see around me. As I am unable to comprehend this alien community, the world before me is often one of commotion, with fish and other animals swirling all around. My photographic approach, one learned over time, is to focus on one behavior or one scene at a time to make order out of chaos. As I begin to assemble in my mind the oceanic puzzle around me, I can then take a broader view, seeing the whole as the sum of its parts. Sharks, however, represent order to my photographic eye, eons of evolution resulting in fluid perfection.

What always strikes me first is the symmetry, the flawless balance that sharks display. Each species has evolved to excel within its habitat. Pelagic sharks such as the oceanic whitetip or blue are designed with long pectoral

the water while its skin, composed of millions of tiny "teeth" called dermal denticles, reduces drag and turbulence, so the shark can swoop in silently on unsuspecting prey.

Different morphologies characterize other species, and I have watched with admiration how beautifully each shark species functions within its home. During an expedition to the remote southern Line Islands in the Pacific, I made sure to be diving at dusk on most days, since this is a time of frenetic activity on the reef. On one such dive I watched in amazement as more than 60 gray reef sharks swirled around me in every direction. It was a primordial experience as I hunkered down among the corals in the warm sea, my eyes adjusting to the dim light, and watched these sharks dominate their world. This is a time of transition on the reef, when daytime animals seek safe refuge for the night and when nocturnal species emerge from the secret places where they slumbered when the sunlight was bright. It seemed as if a switch had been turned on within the sharks, their behavior turning from casual to intense. They were in hunting mode now, and the competition was fierce. To see the sharks during the day was beautiful, almost peaceful, but the scene at sunset was something different. I watched these predators race over corals at speeds I had never seen before, adeptly navigating the uneven terrain, their dorsal fins, tails, and stout pectorals giving them tremendous advantage over every creature within their sphere.

I had a front-row seat to the epitome of evolution, watching the sharks' shape and form function perfectly, resulting in a supreme reign over all they surveyed.

Their senses, likewise fine-tuned through evolution, were totally engaged. Shark eyes are especially good in low light, giving them a clear advantage at this hour, and the electroreceptors they have evolved make them nearly unbeatable. Called ampullae of Lorenzini, these jelly-filled pores dot the snout of sharks and are capable of detecting weak electrical signals. I have seen sharks react to such signals, biting at a boat's propeller, since its bronze, when immersed in seawater, creates a weak electrical field. I have noticed sharks' fascination with my camera's strobes, whose oscillators also emit electrical current. But nature did not design the shark to benefit from metal boat parts or underwater flashes. The ampullae of Lorenzini give sharks the advantage in murky or dark water, because with them they can detect the heartbeat of their prey.

Highly tuned senses capable of detecting both mechanical and electrical stimuli, eyes that adjust exceptionally well in low light, a musculature and specialized dentition—all these attributes make the shark a perfect predator. And then there is their sense of smell. We marvel at the abilities of bears and wolves, able to use smell to track prey over great distances on land. Although there have been highly exaggerated claims about sharks' sense of smell—it is not true that they can smell a drop of blood in the ocean—these animals do have a highly sensitive olfactory system, perfectly adapted to smelling underwater. Depending on the species, some sharks can discern the scent of their prey at one part per 10 billion, which is about one drop in an Olympic-size pool. For an ocean predator constantly searching for food, this is especially helpful. A white shark swimming miles offshore from a seal colony can pick up the diluted scent and home in.

THESE TOP PREDATORY SPECIES are remarkable, but my admiration for sharks extends to the plankton feeders equally. In my native New England waters I have swum alongside massive basking sharks, their gaping mouths open as they charged through nutrient-rich, jade-colored seas. My first experience with such a creature was seeing a whale shark, the basking shark's Southern Hemisphere cousin. Off the coast of western Australia, I quietly slipped into the blue water, finned away from the boat, and waited, staring out into the featureless underwater void. And then it appeared, a hazy apparition that grew into a massive living being before my eyes.

It was a surreal phenomenon, watching this creature swim toward me. There was no sound, only my own heart beating in my chest as this spotted, dirigible-shaped fish, nearly 40 feet long, peacefully passed me by. I swam alongside for as long as I could. The shark seemed to be barely swimming, yet I exerted all the energy I had to keep up. After a few moments I peeled off and watched the whale shark disappear. In the waters of Isla Mujeres, Mexico, I again found whale sharks, but this time I was surrounded by them, for at certain times of the year this place hosts the world's largest gathering of the world's largest fish. They come here to dine on plankton and the tiny eggs from tuna, which spawn here. Day after day I would spend hours free diving with these sharks, and it was like being in the middle of a busy city street, for in every direction I looked I found a passing whale shark.

Having spent the majority of my life exploring the ocean, I am regularly reminded—on every dive—of just how inadequate and poorly designed I am for life underwater. I marvel at all marine creatures and wish I possessed the ability to move effortlessly, as they do, through the sea. But I am most humbled and most in awe of the shark. Producing the most compelling images generally requires me to be close to my subject, yet when I watch them from afar, I see the shark behaving naturally, not affected by my presence. And from this perspective I have come to see them as confident and exceptional, while vulnerable and fragile. They are but one important part of a much grander system, a vital relationship in which all flora and fauna are inexorably entwined. Like the gears of a well-crafted timepiece, all elements of an ecosystem mesh together in harmony, creating a perfectly functioning engine. Each gear, each component relies on another. Remove one part and the engine breaks down. As apex predators in the sea, sharks keep marine ecosystems healthy and vibrant. Nature anointed them to rule, yet they do so in a delicate balance, for everything is connected and everything matters. ∎

Around the world, scientists are finding that healthy coral reef ecosystems, like this one in the Bahamas, are teeming with sharks. All parts of these environments are connected: Caribbean reef sharks need abundant populations of prey, and those smaller fish need their own food, along with coral, anemones, and sponges to hide, mate, lay eggs, and grow in.

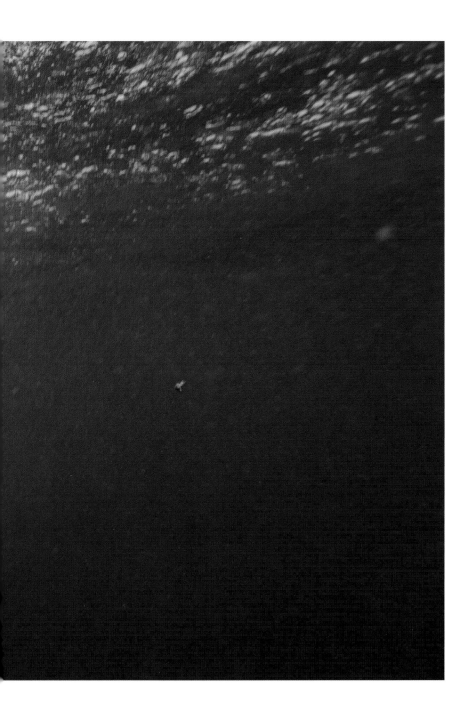

Great white sharks are some of the most amazing creatures I have ever encountered. They barrel through the water when attacking, and their powerful jaws can extend from their bodies, sharp teeth ripping chunks of flesh from prey like whales and other sharks. When they venture into deep water where food is scarce, great whites can rely on fats and oils stored in their livers.

I find myself drawn to the individual body parts of sharks. Millions of years of evolution have crafted the lemon shark's dorsal fin, which steadies the shark as it glides through the water. It also provides a hanging-on place for remoras, small fish that cling to many species of sharks and whales, eating scraps from their hosts' meals.

The basking shark is a massive, filter-feeding shark found throughout the Northern Hemisphere. They swim with their enormous mouths wide open, catching plankton, krill, and other small marine life as they move through the water. I encountered this one far off the coast of Massachusetts.

This mangrove forest in Bimini, Bahamas, is a nursery for lemon shark pups. At only a few weeks old, they are perfect miniatures of adult lemon sharks. The mangrove roots keep them safe from predators during the first few months of their lives, before these sharks head out into open waters. I wanted to capture images of sharks at this vulnerable stage of their lives to help show people that these animals are more than dangerous predators. They're fascinating, multidimensional animals with rich lives.

Bull sharks are one of the most adaptable species of sharks. They're comfortable in water that many other sharks aren't, including brackish and occasionally freshwater. Many search marinas, docks, and other populated areas for scraps left behind by humans. They tend to be aggressive and territorial.

At Isla Holbox in the Gulf of Mexico, whale sharks gather to feed every year. From a boat it seems like these massive fish swim rather slowly, but when I got into the water, I was surprised by their speed. I wanted to swim ahead to capture the living wreath of scad circling this shark's head, and just keeping up took a tremendous effort.

More than 700 islands make up the Bahamas, a diverse array of mangrove forests, coral reefs, sandy flats, and deep waters. In 2011 the Bahamian government made commercial shark fishing illegal in the islands, protecting nearly 250,000 square miles of water. But many of these sharks have wide ranges and roam into unprotected waters where they are put at risk.

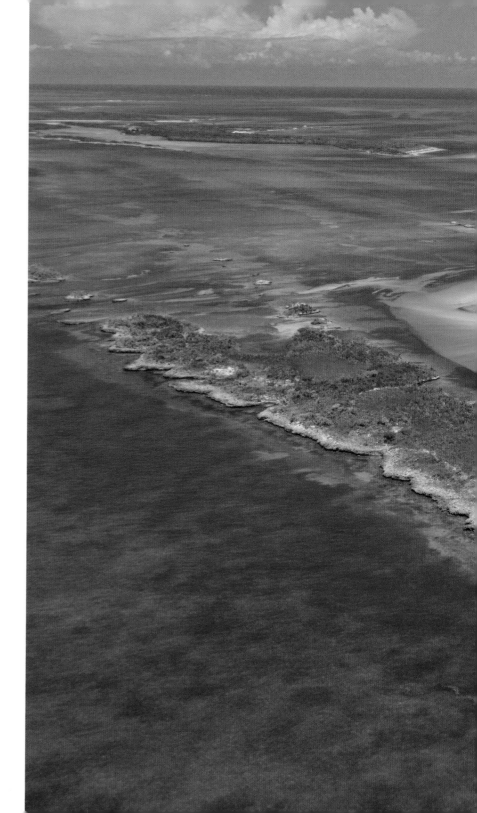

Even on a young mako shark, you can see the how large the tail is in proportion to the rest of its body. That powerful tail helps propel these sharks through the water at breakneck speeds, like a torpedo with teeth. Makos always seem to be hyperaware of their presence in the water—this one just barely lets his dorsal fin break the surface.

All those teeth make the sand tiger shark look mean, but it is one of the politer species of sharks that I have encountered. I met this one near the Ogasawara Islands off the coast of Japan, an area known for its sand tigers.

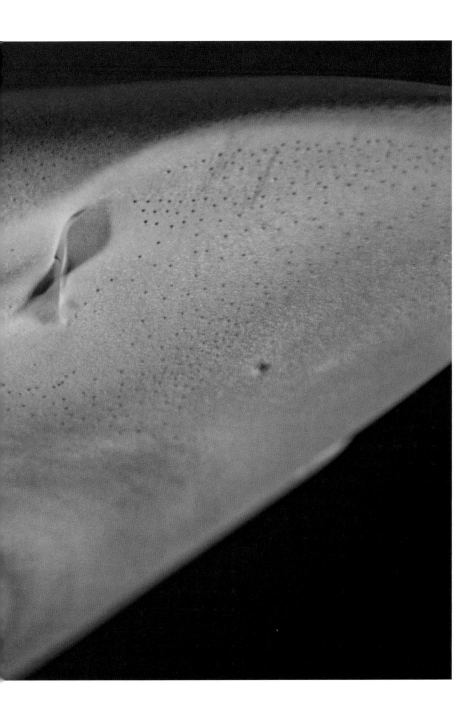

Sharks have incredible eyesight, especially in low-light environments. The iris of this silky shark almost looks like a cat's eye—and for good reason. Cats and sharks both have a mirrorlike layer in the back of their eyes called the tapetum lucidum, a structure that boosts their sensitivity to light.

Walker's Cay in the Bahamas was once home to a large shark-diving operation. Tour guides would anchor a block of frozen fishing scraps (called a chumsicle) to the ocean floor and wait for the sharks to arrive. Here, Caribbean reef sharks and hundreds of smaller fish swarm, worked into a near frenzy by the smell of the chum. Nowadays the island is largely deserted.

Caribbean reef sharks are developing a taste for the invasive lionfish (opposite). Lionfish have no natural predators in the Caribbean, but Honduran scientists are coaching sharks to see them as prey in an effort to control their booming populations. In Mexico a remora investigates the mouth of a whale shark in search of food scraps (above).

At Tiger Beach in the Bahamas, tiger sharks have acclimated to the presence of humans (and know that many will have food for them). Vincent Canabal is an ecotourism guide who works at Tiger Beach and knows many of the sharks here on sight.

CHAPTER TWO

GREAT
WHITE

GREAT WHITE SHARKS— STILL A MYSTERY

They may be the ocean's most iconic and feared fish, and yet we know surprisingly little about them.

ERIK VANCE

Meeting a great white shark in the wild is nothing like you expect it would be. At first glance it's not the malevolent beast we've come to expect from a thousand TV shows. It's portly, bordering on fat, like an overstuffed sausage. Flabby jowls tremble down its body when it opens its mouth, which otherwise is a chubby, slightly parted smirk. From the side, one of the world's greatest predators is little more than a slack-jawed buffoon.

It's only when the underwater clown turns to face you that you understand why it's the most feared animal on earth. From the front its head is no longer soft and jowly but tapers to an arrow that draws its black eyes into a sinister-looking V. The bemused smile is gone, and all you see are rows of two-inch teeth capable of crunching down with almost two tons of force. Slowly, confidently, it approaches you. It turns its head, first to one side and then the other, evaluating you, deciding whether you're worth its time. Then, if you're lucky, it turns away, becoming the buffoon again, and glides lazily into the gloom.

There are more than 400 species of sharks, but in popular imagination there's really only one. When Pixar needed an underwater villain for its animated film *Finding Nemo,* it didn't look to the affable nurse shark or the aggressive bull shark. Not even the tiger shark, which would be more appropriate in Nemo's coral-reef home. It was the great white shark—with its wide, toothy grin—that was plastered on thousands of movie billboards across the world.

The great white shark is the ocean's iconic fish, yet we know little about it—and much of what we *think* we know simply isn't true. White sharks aren't

PREVIOUS PAGES: The Neptune Islands, located off the southern coast of Australia, are one of the world's major hubs for great white activity.

merciless hunters (if anything, attacks are cautious), they aren't always loners, and they may be smarter than experts have thought. Even the 1916 Jersey Shore attacks famously mentioned in *Jaws* may have been perpetrated by a bull shark, not a great white.

We don't know for sure how long they live, how many months they gestate, when they reach maturity. No one has seen great whites mate or give birth. We don't really know how many there are or where, exactly, they spend most of their lives. Imagine that a land animal the size of a pickup truck hunted along the coasts of California, South Africa, and Australia. Scientists would know every detail of its mating habits, migrations, and behavior after observing it in zoos, research facilities, perhaps even circuses. But the rules are different underwater. Great whites appear and disappear at will, making it nearly impossible to follow them in deep water. They refuse to live behind glass—in captivity some have starved themselves or slammed their heads against walls. (Several aquariums have released them for their own safety or because they were attacking tank mates.)

Yet scientists today, using state-of-the-art technologies, may be on the verge of answering two of the most vexing questions: How many are there, and where do they go? Unraveling these mysteries could be critical to deciding how to protect ourselves from them and them from us. When we finally see the great white clearly from all angles, will the world's most fearsome killer deserve our fear or our pity?

A 24-FOOT FISHING BOAT sits just off the southern tip of Cape Cod, Massachusetts, on a perfect summer afternoon. The passengers—three scientists, two paying customers, two journalists, and the boat's captain—lounge on the seats, looking off toward Nantucket. The voice of a spotter pilot flying a thousand feet above breaks out over the radio in a sharp New England accent. "We've got a wicked nice shark over here to the south!"

Fisheries biologist Greg Skomal perks up. He's standing five feet off the bow on the pulpit, a fenced-in walkway resembling a pirate's plank. If this were a Hollywood movie, he'd have a harpoon and a peg leg. Instead he carries a GoPro camera attached to a 10-foot pole. He grins like a little kid as the captain guns the engine.

Before 2004 hardly anyone in modern times saw great white sharks in the waters off the East Coast. Occasionally one would appear near a beach or in a fishing net, but they were anomalies. Elsewhere, great whites congregate seasonally around five "hubs" or territories, including California's coast down to Mexico's Baja California, South Africa's southern shores, and Australia's southern coast, where they gather to feed on seals. But there's been no hub on the East Coast, nor have there been many seals. Sharks here were wanderers without a home. Then, in 2004, a single female found her way into shallow inlets and shoals near Woods Hole, Massachusetts.

For Skomal, who'd been tagging other sharks for 20 years, this was the chance of a lifetime—a great white in his own backyard. "I thought it was a fluke. This will never happen again," he says with his broad, boyish grin under ruffled salt-and-pepper hair. Over the next two weeks Skomal and his colleagues followed the shark, which they named Gretel after the lost girl in the fairy tale, and affixed an electronic tracker on her. Tracking a white shark across the Atlantic Ocean offered a chance to solve so many riddles. But 45 minutes into the journey, Gretel's tag malfunctioned and popped off. "I went from this superhigh to this really deep low, because I was convinced that this was the shot in my career to study a white shark," Skomal says.

It wasn't. Over the next few years he thought a lot about Gretel and wondered whether she was indeed alone. Then, on Labor Day, 2009, everything changed. A pilot saw five great whites off the Cape. Over that weekend Skomal tagged them all. "I absolutely freaked out. My adrenaline was pumping. My heart—I could feel it just pounding in my chest. This was everything I was dreaming of."

White sharks have returned every summer since, leading some to call Cape Cod the sixth hub. How many great whites are there? For that we turn to the hub running from California to Baja California. The effort to count sharks there was pioneered by Scot Anderson while he was a volunteer seabird scientist in the mid-1980s on an island west of San Francisco's Golden Gate Bridge. Anderson and others have tracked the sharks—at first by sight, then by acoustic tags, and most recently with satellites. During the past 30 years, teams have assembled thousands of observations of individual sharks recognized by the shape and marks of their dorsal fins, while others have used the distinctive line between their gray bodies and white underbellies. Scientists know where the sharks congregate and how they feed. And each year most sharks they see are the ones they saw in previous years.

This raised an intriguing question: With enough observations, could you use the sharks you see to estimate how many you can't see? In 2011 a team in California did just that and came up with just 219 adults in California's most shark-rich region. Even among top predators, generally less abundant than their prey, that's a tiny number. The study shocked the public and came under immediate attack from other experts.

Of course, counting great whites is a lot harder than counting land animals or even marine mammals. So scientists make massive assumptions about shark movements and then extrapolate. In California the biggest assumption was that a few feeding grounds were representative of the entire hub. Other teams crunched the same data using different assumptions, and one study estimated about 10 times more sharks. (That count was bolstered by adding juveniles, which the first excluded because so little is known about them.) Pretty soon scientists began quantifying white sharks in the other hubs. A team in South Africa estimated the population there at around 900, while another team put Mexico's Guadalupe Island population, part of the California hub, at just 120 or so.

Are these large numbers or small? Are great whites thriving or dwindling? The world has about 4,000 tigers and 25,000 African lions. Using the lowest estimates, global great white numbers resemble the estimate for tigers, an endangered species. Using the highest estimate, the population is closer to that of the lions, which are classified as vulnerable. Several experts see great whites heading toward extinction; others see a positive trend. Some say rising seal populations are a sign that great whites are nearly gone, while others say more seals mean more sharks. Aaron MacNeil, an Australian statistician who crunches shark data, says the appearance of sharks around Cape Cod and the increased activity in the Southern Hemisphere suggest the latter. "I haven't seen any evidence in the last decade that white sharks

are declining," says MacNeil. "Yes, there is a historical depletion of white sharks. But the story is not that they are going extinct. The story is that they are probably increasing very, very slowly."

There's reason to be hopeful. Few if any fishermen target great whites today, yet a global pact, the Convention on International Trade in Endangered Species (CITES), gives white sharks its second strongest conservation rating because fishermen catch them unintentionally. With numbers so low, even accidental catches can play havoc with the species, which, as a top predator, has an ecologically important role in managing the oceans.

TO UNDERSTAND WHETHER great white sharks need our protection, we must know not only how many there are but also where they go. Their migrations aren't neat, like a bird's or a butterfly's. They're messy, with one hugging the coast while another zigzags hundreds of miles out to sea. Many, but not all, seem to seasonally move between warm and cold water. And the paths seem different for males, females, and juveniles.

Today, with long-term, long-distance tags that can communicate via satellite, scientists are finally getting some clarity. For years scientists have noticed that adult great whites in California and Mexico quit the coast in late fall. Now we know where they go: deep water in the middle of the Pacific Ocean. Why they visit this great white shark "café" remains unclear. "I call it Burning Man for white sharks," says Salvador Jorgensen, a biologist who studies factors that drive great white migration and ecology. "They are heading out to what some people call the desert of the ocean, and what the hell are they doing out there?"

One possible answer is mating, which might explain why no one has ever observed it. The area is roughly the size of California and thousands of feet deep, which makes it hard to monitor sharks there. But satellite tags tell us that the females swim predictable straight patterns while the males swim up and down in the water column, possibly searching for mates. Thus a rough sketch of the lives of California white sharks is forming. After spending the summer and fall gorging on seals, they head out to the deep ocean to breed, relying on energy stores to live. The males then swim back to the coast while the females wander to unknown places, where they remain for another year or so, perhaps to birth their young. Newborn sharks then show up at feeding grounds—say, the waters off Southern California—devouring fish until they are big enough to join their elders in the north or south hunting seals.

It's not a perfect picture. Females and males aren't in the café together for long, and we don't know where the babies are born. But it explains a lot. For example, as a population rebounds, its young become plentiful, which is likely why Southern Californians have encountered a lot of sharks lately. Yet it's tougher to figure out elsewhere. Australian sharks forage along the southern coast but don't seem to have a pattern or café. And in the Atlantic we know even less. "We've got wanderers, and we've got coastal sharks. And what dictates which, I have no idea," Skomal says.

sharp eyes can spot them from the air. In just 30 minutes of flying we see seven, all patrolling beaches where gray seals are foraging in open waters. On the way back Davis and I fly past several beaches a mile or so to the north packed with vacationers.

So far locals have embraced their new neighbors. There are stuffed animals, T-shirts, posters, and a community art exhibit called "Sharks in the Park." Even the new high school's mascot is a great white. Most of the time the sharks are shown from the side—cheerful, buffoonish. Experts warn, though, that at some point someone here will meet the other version—the one with teeth.

Attacks on people are incredibly rare. In waters off California, the chances of a surfer being bitten by a great white shark are one in 17 million; for swimmers, it's even rarer—one attack in every 738 million beach visits,

THEIR MIGRATIONS AREN'T NEAT, LIKE A BIRD'S OR A BUTTERFLY'S. THEY'RE MESSY, WITH ONE HUGGING THE COAST WHILE ANOTHER ZIGZAGS HUNDREDS OF MILES OUT TO SEA.

Even though he doesn't understand their migrations yet, Skomal is sure that white sharks have a long history here. At his office in New Bedford, just west of Cape Cod, he opens a document that compiled studies of seal bones from Native American archaeological sites along the eastern seaboard. The discarded bones suggest that seal populations crashed from overhunting perhaps a century before the Declaration of Independence. In other words, we've had very few Atlantic gray seals throughout the United States' 240-year history. Today, thanks to the Marine Mammal Protection Act, seal colonies now populate New England. And when the seals returned, the sharks came home as well.

ONE BRIGHT AUGUST MORNING I board a two-seater plane with Wayne Davis, a veteran spotter pilot for tuna and swordfish who now helps scientists track down white sharks. Unlike the hubs, the water here is so shallow that

according to a recent Stanford University study. On Cape Cod, fatalities may not be a question of if, but when. The last lethal shark attack off New England was in 1936, but there have been several close calls recently. A swimmer there was bitten on both legs in 2012, and two paddlers in Plymouth were knocked from their kayaks in 2014, although they escaped unscathed. If a more serious attack happens, Massachusetts will join the other hubs in weighing the benefits versus the dangers of sharks in their waters.

It may be that great white sharks are rebounding across the world: following the bigger seal and sea lion populations, reestablishing themselves in their old hunting grounds, reclaiming the coasts they nearly lost.

Then again, it may be that great whites today are hanging over the abyss of extinction, clutching the edge by the skin of their jagged teeth. Will we look past our fear and reach out a hand to this creature? Can we take pity on the pitiless eyes of a monster? ■

Great whites are usually solitary animals, but in hubs like the Neptune Islands they can be found in groups, especially near feeding grounds. During this dive I saw sharks on every side. Between the hazy water and the schools of silverfish, visibility was low, and I was surprised when one shark swam right up to my cage and pressed her face against my camera.

Like other sharks, great whites have sharp low-light vision, and many actively hunt and patrol as the sun sets. In the Neptune Islands, schools of silver jacks swim alongside sharks, something that you don't see often. They're not a fish that great whites are terribly interested in eating and may be used as cover while the sharks hunt larger prey.

Greg Skomal has been studying sharks for more than
20 years. When a new population of great whites emerged
in Massachusetts in the early 2000s, he was ecstatic. He is
studying the Cape Cod population with a variety of methods.
Here, he's recording a white shark swimming near Nauset
Beach, one of the most popular on the Cape.

This shot is from my first season working on the Cape, while I was trying to figure out the best way to capture these truly wild sharks. They weren't interested in any of our bait, and the Cape's shallow, murky water and strong currents made underwater shots especially challenging.

They spend a lot of time out in the open ocean, but great whites live in a diverse array of habitats. For me, seeing them swim through places like this kelp forest in the Neptune Islands offers a brief glimpse at the richness of their lives and experiences.

Satellite tagging provides scientists with new understanding of the great white's impressive migration. Sharks that spend the summer and fall off the coast of California head out to deep water in the central Pacific in the winter and spring, to an area scientists call the great white café. So far, Australian sharks like this one don't seem to have a similar pattern.

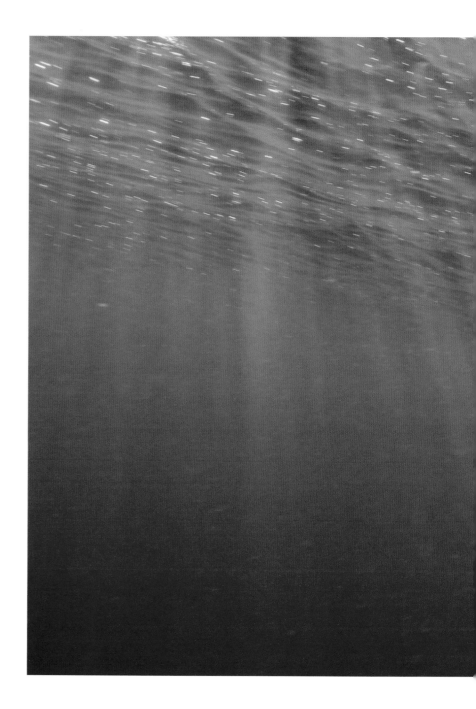

Cape Cod white sharks have a singular focus on seals. Since the
1972 Marine Mammal Protection Act banned seal hunting, their
numbers have been steadily increasing. As they have returned to
places like Monomoy Island (opposite), so have the sharks. I built
seal decoys with cameras inside to get close to sharks like this one,
which I nicknamed Mike Tyson because of the scars on his face.

Chatham is the epicenter of great white activity in Cape Cod, though as the sharks become more abundant their range is expanding across the Massachusetts coast. Other shark species—blue sharks, basking sharks, shortfin makos—are found in the area, but great whites are the only ones hunting in the sandy waters close to shore. Their emergence in this area is like a new pride of lions emerging in the Serengeti.

In Australia these small silver jacks would sometimes
school underneath a shark, occasionally coming up to
bump up against the shark's rough skin. Like other
smaller fish species, they may be using the shark as a
form of protection. They're too small for a shark this size
to have much interest in eating them, but larger fish that
might make dinner of them are too wary to venture close.

Because the Cape Cod sharks aren't interested in anything other than seals, we had the challenging task of developing a convincing seal decoy to get their attention. After my first attempt at a decoy didn't work, I worked with a veterinarian to build a smaller, more realistic fake seal that managed to draw the sharks' attention.

In the shallow waters of the Cape, great whites attack
differently than we've seen in the open ocean. The attack
is a newly documented behavior in white sharks—
they will bite their prey at the surface, then back
off and allow it to bleed to death.

It might appear that this great white is chasing down a tiny snack, but this small silver jack isn't something a shark is particularly interested in. You see this with a lot of larger sharks—small fish swim just in front of their noses, like dolphins swimming at the front of a boat. The jack may be taking advantage of how the larger fish cuts through the water, making it easier to swim.

A great white trolls the surface off the southern coast of Australia at dusk. Like people, many sharks have routines that bring them to different parts of the ocean at different times of day. As we learn more about sharks' behavior and habits, we're starting to understand that these animals are more than the dangerous predators that many people think of them as.

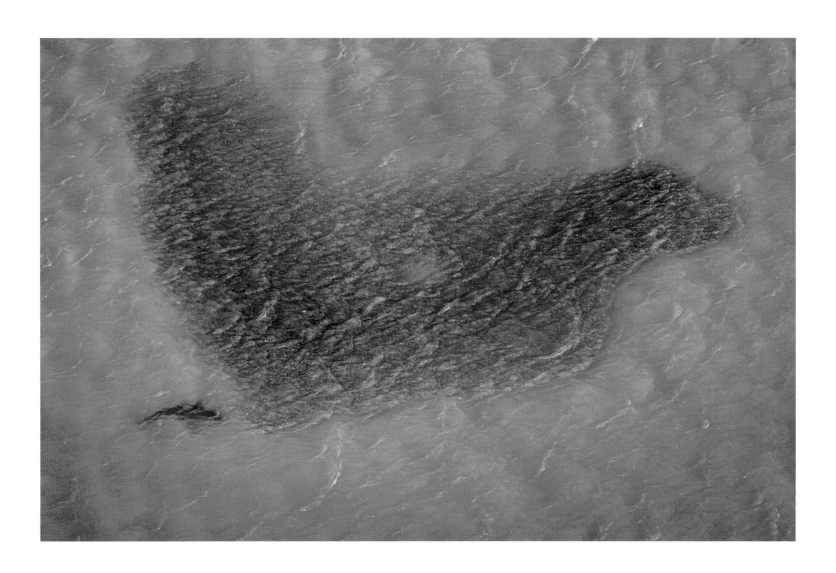

Guadalupe Island is one of the other hubs of great white activity. I took this photo (opposite) in 1998 on my first trip there. It's a mecca for divers looking to experience great whites up close. In the newly emerging hub at Cape Cod (above), great whites will ignore large schools of fish, like these menhaden, in search of gray seals.

Great whites are opportunist predators, and most will eat anything from large fish (including other sharks) to whales, dolphins, seals, sea turtles, and seabirds. In different parts of the world, white sharks show different preferences, often based on the prey that's available in a particular region. In Australia, where this photograph was made, they're often seen eating seals and sea lions.

Even at Tiger Beach sharks tend to be initially cautious around humans. They approach slowly and often investigate by bumping divers with their noses. As the sharks become acclimated to humans, they become friendlier and visit the area regularly. On any given day Tiger Beach will have multiple tiger sharks waiting at the bottom. This shark also had its sensitive eyes closed, to protect them from sand and debris on the ocean floor.

When I set out to make photographs of tiger sharks,
I wanted to emulate their terrestrial namesakes.
Like a tiger slinking through tall grass in the jungle,
this tiger shark approaches from behind a purple sea
fan. The lush sea grasses on the ocean floor provide
cover for sharks hunting in these shallow waters.

A tiger shark's mouth is an impressive thing, as I saw firsthand when one started investigating my camera with its mouth. With wide jaws and heavy serrated teeth, these sharks have been known to bite through license plates, paint cans, and other debris—they're not particularly picky eaters.

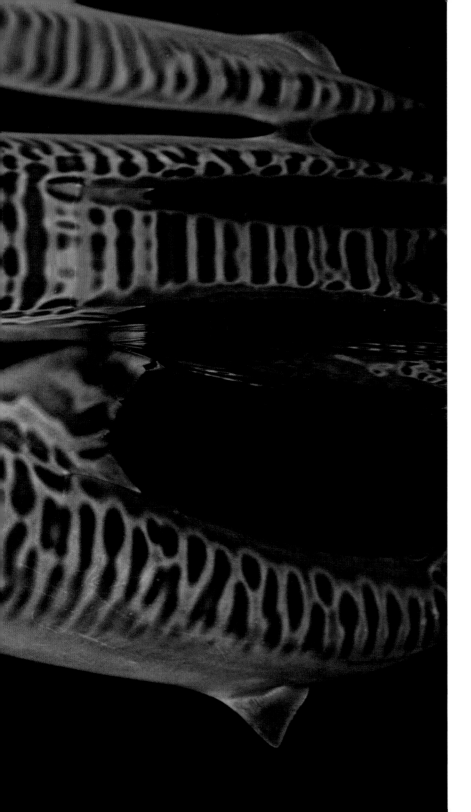

Nobody has ever seen a shark mate or give birth (with the exception of nurse sharks), and even finding young sharks can be difficult. Carl Meyer, a shark biologist at the University of Hawaii, found this four- or five-day-old tiger shark. Its distinctive stripes are brighter than an adult's and will fade with age. I believe that the more we learn about sharks, the more we will be able to empathize with them—and work harder to protect them.

The ocean floor in the Bahamas is littered with the evidence of old wrecks, like this anchor chain from an unknown ship. Tiger sharks hang out near many of these shipwrecks and, along with small reef fish, have colonized these remnants from human travelers, transforming them into their own habitats.

On my first trip to Tiger Beach I met this female tiger shark (opposite). A couple of bar jacks swam in front of her as she rose to the surface, creating a shadow on her face. The tiger sharks in South Africa (above) were a completely different story—they're wild in a way the sharks at Tiger Beach have not been for years.

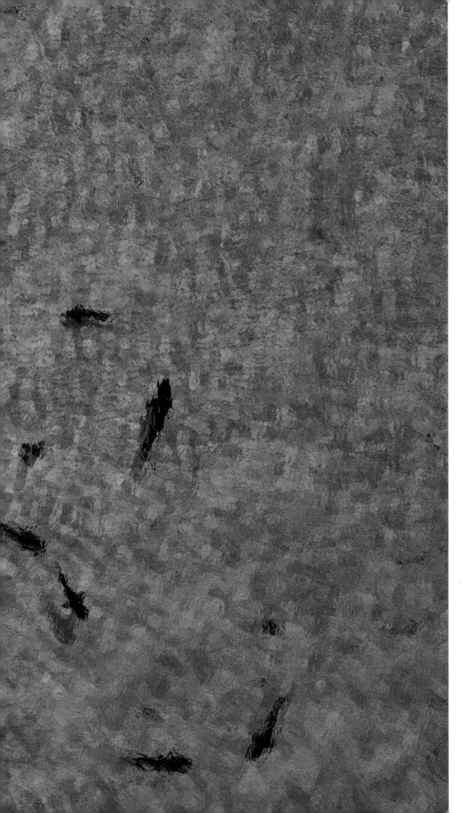

Calm, clear waters and low winds really showcase the shark presence on Tiger Beach. Each of these sharks is about 12 to 14 feet long—many of them are females who spend their pregnancies in the warm waters of the Bahamas. I made this photograph using a camera attached to a blimp (you can see the tether attaching it to the boat on the left side of the image).

Tiger sharks patrol the water column, passing through shallow and deep environments in search of prey. They're the ultimate tropical predator: resilient, adaptable sharks that play a key role as apex predators. Some of the hot spots for tiger sharks overlap with centers of human activity, giving them a reputation as particularly dangerous sharks.

Relying on stealth, tiger sharks are ambush predators that come from below to attack prey at the water's surface. Their powerful bodies can surge toward the surface to catch an unwitting fish or sea turtle by surprise.

Swimming with tiger sharks in South Africa, I felt like I was
part of the food web in a way that I didn't in the Bahamas.
I worked with Ryan Daly, a shark researcher at Rhodes
University in South Africa, to track down this large male tiger.

You can see a bit of food from a dive operator at Tiger Beach inside this tiger's mouth, but almost none of its razor-sharp teeth are currently showing. When they attack living prey, tiger sharks' jaws can cut through just about anything—one shark was found with an entire suit of armor in its stomach.

Photographing sharks, especially ones that aren't acclimated to humans like the tigers in South Africa, can be dangerous. When I see a shark out in the blue void, I'm often praying that it'll come close enough for me to capture an image. But sometimes as they approach, my heart will start to race and I'll wonder what I've gotten myself into. This shark looks like it's in an aggressive posture, but when it approached, it didn't give me any trouble.

One tiger in South Africa had something that I haven't seen anywhere else in the world: an entourage of remoras (opposite). Normally these small fish cling to the shark's body, taking advantage of the shark's top predator status. Remoras are opportunists that often latch onto sharks when they're moving slowly, like these sharks in the Bahamas (above).

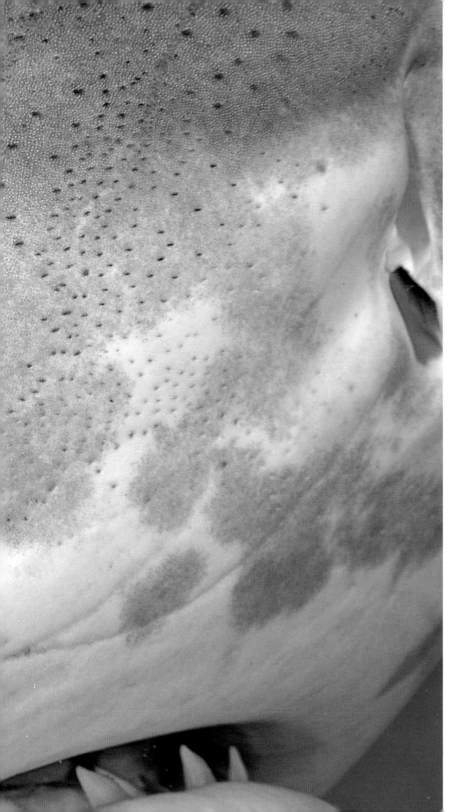

Part of why sharks are such efficient predators lies in their finely tuned senses. Like other sharks, tigers have good low-light vision. They also have jelly-filled nerve endings on their snouts, called the ampullae of Lorenzini (the small dots behind the nostrils). These allow them to detect electrical signals and home in on nearby prey. Sharks also have exceptional senses of smell, and specialized teeth round out an already impressive lineup.

Sharks with hooks and fishing lines trailing from their mouths like this female tiger shark have become a common sight in the Bahamas. Commercial shark fishing is illegal there, but when fishermen reel in sharks, many don't feel like they can safely remove the hooks before releasing them back into the wild.

CHAPTER FOUR

SHORTFIN MAKO

A SHORT COURSE ON WHY TO SAVE THE MAKO

The shortfin mako may be the fastest shark in the North Atlantic, but can it outswim our appetites for meat and sport?

GLENN HODGES

Two summers ago I spent a long day aboard a fishing boat some 30 miles off the coast of Ocean City, Maryland, observing shortfin mako sharks being caught and tagged with satellite transmitters. I watched as the fishermen on board reeled in two young makos and scientists tagged the larger of the two, a five-and-a-half-footer that weighed about a hundred pounds. It was quite a scene, so much so that I went out again in Rhode Island later in the summer. And there I noticed something interesting.

On each trip I was accompanying scientists affiliated with the Guy Harvey Research Institute, which has been tagging and tracking shortfin makos in the Atlantic Ocean and Gulf of Mexico for years. The excursions out of Ocean City were a resounding success, with multiple makos caught and fitted with satellite transmitters capable of tracking their whereabouts for years. The Rhode Island excursions were an equally resounding failure: one week, zero makos. So why am I glad I went? Because sometimes you learn more from what you don't see than from what you do.

ONE OF THE FIRST THINGS you learn when you're fishing for makos is that they share territory with blue sharks. The two species are kind of like lions and hyenas, coexisting in the same areas as they pursue different feeding strategies. Shortfin makos are the fastest sharks in the ocean, capable of chasing down speedy prey like bluefish and tuna. They are distinguished from their much rarer cousins, longfin makos, by, among other things, their shorter pectoral fins. Sport fishermen love them. Explosively powerful, they put up a great fight on the line, sometimes jumping several feet in the air, and they're extraordinarily good to eat, rivaling swordfish in meat quality. Blue sharks, on the other hand, are relatively laconic, and they focus on slower prey, like jellyfish. As one fisherman put it, catching them is like "reeling in a barn door," and their meat is not especially good to eat. So you can guess, in the analogy, which one is the lion and which the hyena. Everyone wants to bag the lion—which is to say, shortfin makos are the fisherman's mark. On our second day out of Narragansett, as we reeled yet another blue shark to the side of the boat, I finally took note of the obvious.

"It seems like all the blue sharks have hooks in their mouths," I said.

Brad Wetherbee, the marine ecologist from the University of Rhode Island who was there to tag any makos we caught, said, "Yup. Every one we've brought back to the boat so far has had a hook in it."

Removing a hook from a shark's mouth can be dangerous, so when fishermen reel in a species that doesn't interest them, they simply cut the leader lines and leave the hooks to slowly rust away. I'd already noticed that blue sharks were more likely to have hooks in their mouths than makos. "I've never seen a mako with a hook," the ship's mate, Lucas Berg, told me our first day out. "People don't ever let them go. But we've caught blue sharks with four hooks in their mouth."

The fishing pressures on shortfin makos are intense, Wetherbee explained. They migrate northward up the Atlantic coast in the summer, and between everyday recreational fishing and the dozens of shark-fishing tournaments held between Maryland and Rhode Island, it's like running a gantlet. "Certainly a lot of them have been weeded out by the time they get up here," Wetherbee said.

I knew that makos, like many sharks, are especially vulnerable to overfishing because of their small litters and high age at which they reach sexual maturity. The International Union for Conservation of Nature (IUCN) considers them overfished on a global level. Makos are not only targets for recreational fishermen; they are frequently snagged as bycatch by tuna longliners and caught deliberately besides. Between the value of their fins (prized in Asia for shark fin soup) and the value of their meat, they're under significant pressure.

"Is the catch rate sustainable?" I asked Wetherbee.

"We don't know," he said. "These are far-ranging, international sharks—some of our makos have gone into the waters of 16 different countries—and there's not enough data for management agencies to come up with a good estimate of whether the population is going up, or down, or staying the same. There's probably some number of mako sharks that would be fine to catch and kill. But we don't know if it's a hundred, or a thousand, or a hundred thousand."

What they do know is that the sharks they're tagging are not faring well. The tags they use—mounted on the dorsal fin, about the size of a cigarette pack—send signals to satellites every time the sharks wearing them surface, allowing them to create detailed maps of their movements. When the signals start coming from land, they know the sharks have been caught. "We've tagged 49 makos, and 11 have been killed." (Within a month, that number had increased to 12.) I said that seemed like a lot to me, and he agreed: The sample size is small, but the catch rate is alarming.

Back on land I called Mahmood Shivji, the Nova Southeastern University scientist who is the lead researcher of the tagging project, to ask him about the catch rate of the sharks they'd tagged. "What amazes me," he said, "is that it's a vast ocean out there and these animals move a lot, and yet these satellite-tagged animals are running into fishing hooks to the tune of 25 percent—which is pretty staggering, I think. No shark fishery can sustain a 25 percent removal every year."

According to the National Marine Fisheries Service (NMFS), which regulates fishing in U.S. waters, shortfin makos are being fished at a sustainable level, he said. "I will tell you, though," he added, "that the quality of data that goes into stock assessments is a problem, because those stock assessments are based on commercial fisheries' catch data, and the accuracy of that data is questionable at best."

Both Shivji and Wetherbee referred me to Enric Cortés, who evaluates fishery data and makes stock assessments for NMFS, which then are used to set fishing regulations. They both said they respected him and thought he did a good job with the data he had, but when I called Cortés he readily admitted that the data available to him for mako sharks were insufficient. "It looks like the population is OK, but we're not really sure," he said. And by "not really sure" he meant not sure at all.

Until NMFS has better data at its disposal, it's unlikely to change fishing regulations because, as Shivji puts it, "It takes a very dire situation for NMFS to shut down a fishery, because the political pushback is huge." At present, the minimum size for a legally caught shark, any species, is 54 inches, which is well under the size at which makos reach sexual maturity. In 2012 the agency proposed larger size limits to protect juveniles of vulnerable species, but ultimately NMFS backed down. Still, the data from Shivji's study might be a step in that direction. Although the original intent of the tagging study was to examine makos' movement patterns, the high catch rate of their tagged sharks has prompted another conclusion: It appears that shortfin makos in the North Atlantic are being overfished.

TWO WEEKS AFTER those two outings, I returned to Ocean City for Mako Mania, an annual shark-fishing tournament. Ocean City's Mako Mania should not be confused with the Mako Mania tournament in Point Pleasant, New Jersey—or, for that matter, with the Mako Fever tournament in New Jersey, or the Mako Rodeo tournament, also in New Jersey; or with the Block Island Giant Shark Tournament or the Monster Shark Tournament, both in Rhode Island; or with any of the other some 60 to 70 U.S. tournaments that include prizes for hauling in large pelagic (open ocean) sharks like makos, threshers, and tiger sharks. Though the first shark-fishing tournament preceded *Jaws* by a few years, shark fishing boomed after the 1975 movie, and tournaments popped up like mushrooms all over the eastern seaboard. Ever since, summer has not been a good time to be a shark in the North Atlantic.

I arrived at Ocean City's Bahia Marina just as the first sharks were being brought in to the docks. It was a festive scene—hundreds of people drinking and eating and cheering for the anglers and their kills. (It struck me right away that shark fishermen are not shy about the fact that they kill the sharks they catch; they do not use euphemisms like "take" or "harvest.") Next to me a woman and a young boy watched as a 281-pound shortfin mako—the winner in the mako category, it turned out—was hoisted to be weighed. The anglers pulled up the nose for photographs, and the woman turned to the boy and said, "This is really cool, right?" The boy nodded silently, transfixed by the shark's bloody, toothy grimace. Behind that shark, the cleaners were busy cutting apart the mako brought earlier—first lopping the fins off, then gutting it, then cutting the head off and carving the jaw out of the head, and reducing the rest of the shark to filets and chum within minutes.

As the sharks continued rolling in—146-pound mako, 465-pound thresher, 500-pound thresher, 174-pound mako—I talked to the tournament's organizer, Shawn Harman. "What's more fun than seeing sharks?" he asked, surveying the cheering crowd. Soon we got to some of the knottier questions about the controversy over "kill tournaments," as critics call them, versus "no kill" or "catch and release" tournaments, which are rare but do exist. He explained that his tournament was not like the tournaments of old, back in the '70s and '80s, when the sharks would just be piled up on the docks and get thrown wholesale into the Dumpster. At this tournament, only threshers and makos, the best-tasting sharks in the ocean, qualify, and contestants have to observe the rules about minimum sizes and one fish per boat per day. "Nobody's wantonly killing fish here," said Harman. "Everyone here eats what they kill." I asked him where I might find mako on the menu, to see what it tastes like. He fetched a filet from one of the sharks just brought in, had it blackened and grilled, and served it to me on a bun with wasabi mayo. It was delicious—as good as any billfish I'd ever had.

But the tasty sandwich and the festivity of the scene at the Bahia Marina could not entirely conceal the problematic nature of the event. Later in the day I was talking to one of the anglers, who told me that a 500-pound thresher shark brought in earlier that day had been pregnant. When it was gutted, he said, the tournament staff tried to hide the pups from the crowd. Threshers, like makos, are considered "vulnerable" by the IUCN, and killing the pregnant females of vulnerable species is, at the very least, bad publicity.

I asked Harman about the pregnant shark. He denied the story, so I asked one of the guys cleaning the fish, and he said yes, there had indeed been a three-foot pup. I went back to Harman to ask him why he had lied about it. He got a little flustered and told me he was afraid of being the "bad guy" in the story. One year a while back the Society for the Prevention of Cruelty to Animals (SPCA) had released a critical video about the tournament, he said, and it left a bad taste in his mouth. "We're following the law, according to what the law says is sustainable," he said. "If they make it illegal, we'll stop."

THE CAPTAINS OF THE FISHING BOATS I went out in for those tagging operations in Maryland and Rhode Island are both longtime shark fishermen. They are not reflexively against the capture and killing of fish, and they are not squeamish about what deep-sea fishing entails. But both men have qualms about how sharks are presently being fished.

Mark Sampson, the Maryland captain, started a prominent shark-fishing tournament in Ocean City in 1981 and ran it for years. But over time he became increasingly concerned about the conservation of shark populations. He made his size limits more restrictive, to reduce the number of sharks brought needlessly to the dock, and he insisted that anglers use circle hooks, which, in contrast to conventional J hooks, don't pierce the shark's stomach when swallowed and thus result in fewer unnecessary killings. Fishermen

It did, he said, and he started trying to persuade his customers to release the sharks they caught. "I'd tell people, a hundred-pound mako is just a tot, just a kid, because they have the potential to grow to a thousand pounds or more." But given that almost all of the makos they catch out there are juveniles, it stopped making sense to even ask the anglers to decide what to do when they hauled in a hundred-pound shark. In 2015 he instituted a catch-and-release policy, no exceptions—and his business has taken a hit.

Donilon accepts the loss of business because it doesn't seem to him that the current level of shark fishing is sustainable, no matter what the government says. "The sharks we tag, there's like a gantlet they have to go through coming up the coast. They've got to go through Maryland, New Jersey, Long Island, Rhode Island, Massachusetts—and everyone in the world is out there

MAKOS, LIKE MANY SHARKS, ARE ESPECIALLY VULNERABLE TO OVERFISHING BECAUSE OF THEIR SMALL LITTERS AND HIGH AGE AT WHICH THEY REACH SEXUAL MATURITY.

balked and participation declined. Because of the higher size limits, he said, "we had days in our tournament where not a single shark was brought back to the dock. And that's not the recipe for a successful tournament, because people want to see those fish being brought in and weighed." He shuttered his tournament in 2014, and he no longer charters his boat for anglers who want to participate in other shark tournaments.

Charlie Donilon, the Rhode Island captain, has run shark-fishing charters since 1976. Where Sampson is quiet and circumspect, Donilon is talkative and emotional, and on one of those days in August when we were on the boat waiting (and waiting, and waiting) for the fish to bite, he told me about the time they reeled in a mako that didn't want to die.

"I threw a harpoon in it, then I hit it with a flying gaffe, and then tied it down to a side cleat, and the thing is scratching and blasting blood everywhere, and it's all being recorded. The guy sent me the video and I watched it with my wife, and she asked, 'Does that bother you?'"

fishing," he said. "They've got to be 15 years old and 500 pounds in order to reproduce, the females. Now, what are the odds of that shark making it up here 15 times without being caught? Pretty slim."

I thought of all the blue sharks we'd seen with hooks in their mouths, and it seemed to me he was right: pretty slim. Though most casualties tracked through the tagging study were killed by commercial fishermen in international waters, not by recreational fishermen, NMFS statistics attribute many of the mako kills in the United States to recreational fishermen.

So what do the data mean? Who's fishing too much where? It's still too soon to say. The tagging study's sample size is small, and NMFS's statistics are patchy. But Donilon, at least, doesn't need to wait for more data. "I did my share of killing," he said to me one afternoon on the boat. He compared himself to a poacher in Africa who used to kill lions but had a change of heart, and as he did this his eyes teared up and his voice started quivering, and finally he choked out in a half whisper: "We just take, take all the time." ∎

Giant kelp forests along the Pacific coast of North America are home to unparalleled biodiversity. When kelp breaks off and floats to the surface, it can form a drifting kelp paddy that houses a mini-ecosystem within its leaves. Sharks and other large fish are drawn to the prospect of easy food. Here, a mako swims underneath one of these massive kelp paddies off the coast of California.

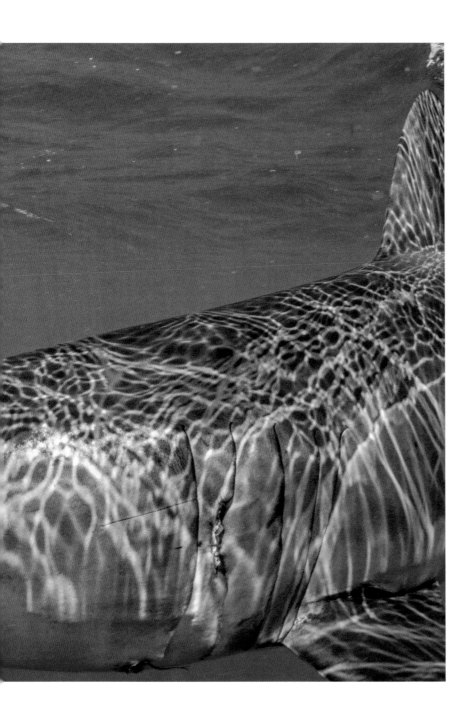

Makos are abundant in New Zealand, compared to the rest of the world's oceans. They tend to lead solitary lives, so it's rare to see multiple makos together. Off of New Zealand's North Island I saw groups multiple times— once nearly 20 in the same place.

Being in the water with mako sharks is exhilarating and exhausting. They're smart, quick sharks, and you have to stay vigilant when one is around, much less three. I was free diving with these makos and had to stay on my toes to keep track of where they were.

Makos are some of the fastest animals in the ocean, with bodies built like a bullet to reduce drag in the water. They can swim in short bursts of up to 45 miles an hour, and even their cruising speed is fast—makos can travel more than 60 miles in a single day.

Strong, capable predators, mako sharks are well equipped for life throughout the water column. Their eyes are larger than many other shark species, allowing them to hunt effectively in deep water where sunlight doesn't reach. I like to call this image "the last thing a tuna sees."

129

With their superior low-light vision, makos take advantage of the dim light of sunset for hunting. This is my favorite time of day to photograph sharks, when they're active and I can capture their true colors with a little added light. I ran into this mako off the coast of Rhode Island as the late summer sun was setting in the background.

Most fishes, including most sharks, are ectothermic, meaning their body temperature matches the temperature of the water. But makos, along with a few other species, are partially endothermic, meaning they can generate their own body heat. This allows them to swim into deeper, darker, colder waters that many other sharks wouldn't survive in for long.

Some sharks check out new things in their surroundings with a nudge of the nose or a bump on the side. Makos like to investigate with their teeth. Their bites aren't always meant as attacks; biting is just how they learn about the world around them. Often once they discover that what they're biting isn't food, they'll move along.

Like tiger sharks, makos are ambush predators. They sneak up from below and take a chunk of their prey—a tuna or a bluefish, sometimes a dolphin. Then they'll let it bleed out until it's too weak to fight back and drag it to deep water to feed.

137

In nearly all of the world's waters you find copepods, small crustaceans that float in the open water or live on the ocean floor. About half of the 13,000 known species of copepods are parasites that attach themselves to marine animals. On this mako shark you can see parasitic copepods attached to the dorsal fin, trailing behind as it swims.

I'm rarely inside a cage when swimming with sharks (except when great whites are around), and often I'm alone. From a safety standpoint, this is a risky move. Some sharks get spooked when there are multiple people in the water, so it's better to be alone if I want to get close. But it's hard to tell when a shark might get aggressive, and those are the times that you want another person in the water to help.

Makos have a reputation as aggressive sharks, which is part of what makes people see them as such a prize catch. But these efficient, elegant predators are declining in number. In New Zealand they're seen as a good eating fish (though more often picked up as bycatch rather than targeted fishing).

143

Around the world, oceanic whitetips are accompanied by pilot fish. By hanging around larger predators, pilot fish ensure that nothing bigger is coming along to eat them. In exchange for this protection, the pilot fish pick parasites off the shark and sometimes even clean bits of food out of the shark's teeth.

The distinctive white tips of this species may have evolved
as a way to attract prey. In the dark waters where oceanic
whitetips hunt, the rest of their bodies are nearly invisible
to passing fish. The white tips of their fins, though, stand out
like a school of small fish that may entice passersby.

I find that oceanic whitetips are intensely curious, possibly because they encounter other animals so infrequently. Once something new enters their space, they rush over and start investigating. They will often bounce their noses on my camera, and I push them off to remind them that I'm not food for them to scavenge.

About 10 years ago I started to hear rumors that oceanic whitetips were stealing marlin and tuna from fishermen near Cat Island in the Bahamas. I hired a boat to investigate, and on that first trip we only encountered a single one over 16 days. It turned out that we had gone at the wrong time of year—the sharks congregate near Cat Island during the spring. When we came back in April and May, we found a small but healthy population of the sharks.

Cat Island is at the edge of a continental shelf, where the shallow coast abruptly drops off into deep water. This is where oceanic whitetips thrive. Shallow water sharks such as dusky sharks, on the right side of the image, sometimes overlap in territory, though duskies prefer the warmer water around reefs.

I first encountered an oceanic whitetip near Cat Island in 2006, with my mentor Wes Pratt (above). Since then I've been lucky to swim with and photograph many more of these beautiful pelagic sharks (opposite).

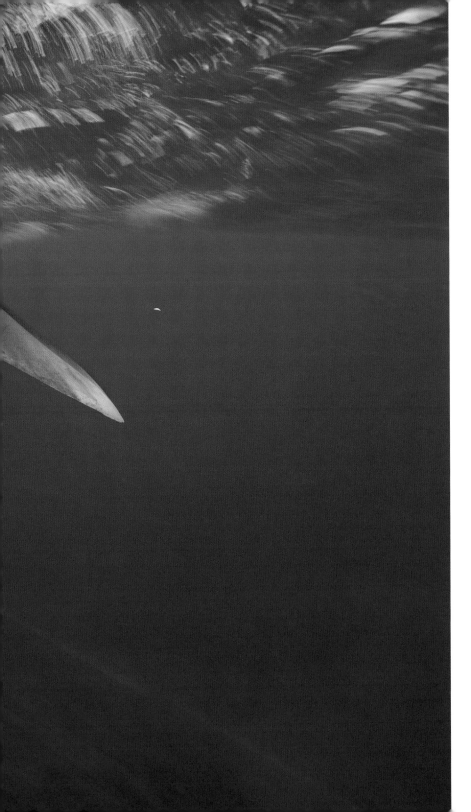

Oceanic whitetip sharks are considered the fourth most dangerous species of shark in the world, after great whites, bull sharks, and tiger sharks. They're admirable predators, of course, like many sharks, but have earned a reputation as killers because they're often found near shipwrecks. Oceanic whitetips have been seriously overfished and their stocks dramatically depleted worldwide.

The scientific name for oceanic whitetips is *Carcharhinus longimanus,* which translates to "long hands" for their long pectoral fins. They're solitary sharks, expending very little energy as the traverse the open ocean. Oceanic whitetips are found in temperate oceans around the world and tend to stay in areas with deep water.

With its winglike pectoral fins, the oceanic whitetip
is built to glide easily through vast expanses of empty
ocean in search of prey. When it finds something that
might be edible, it investigates relentlessly.

Scientists use satellite tags to learn more about
the movement and migration of oceanic whitetips.
We know so little about these sharks, and outside of
the protected waters of the Bahamas they're at risk.
If we can learn more about their habits and habitats,
we can make efforts to protect those areas.

Before that first trip to Cat Island in 2006, I had no experience with oceanic whitetips and could only base my expectations on rumors about these man-killing sharks. We brought along a shark cage, but I felt perfectly safe swimming alongside them in the open water.

Like the numbers for other species of sharks, oceanic whitetip numbers are in decline. The population that frequents Cat Island may be as small as 300 sharks, and it's one of the largest groups known today. While sharks benefit from a commercial fishing ban in the Bahamas, their range expands far beyond Bahamian waters, and if we want to keep these sharks around they're going to need more protections.

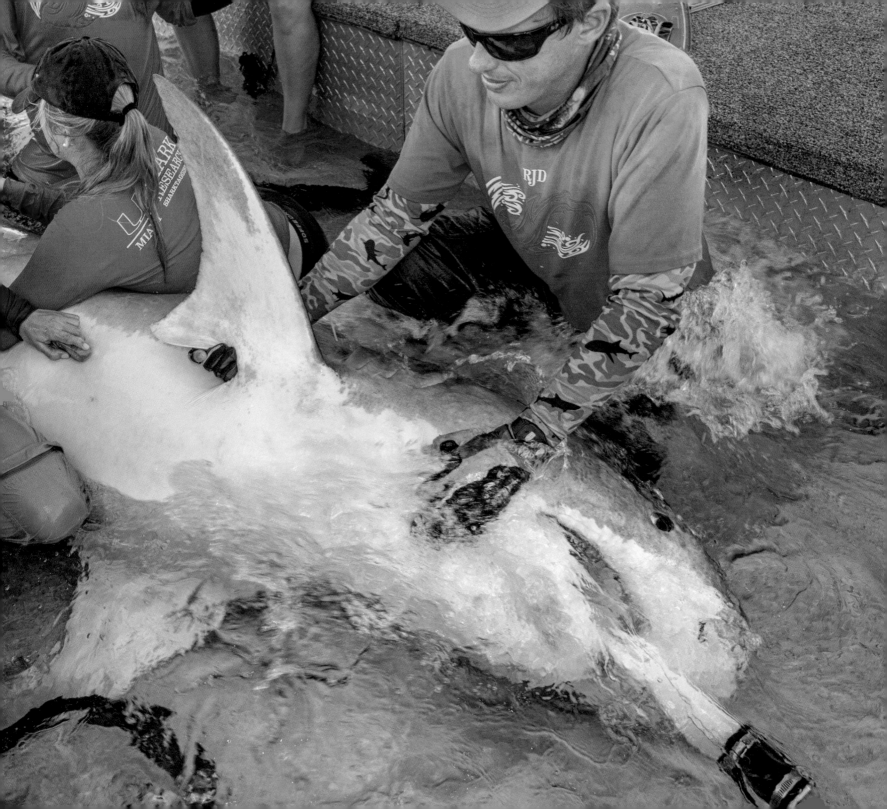

Sportfishing takes enormous skill, but I don't like tournaments
that celebrate and award prizes for the death of sharks.
These animals are important to the health of the ocean,
and I want to find a way to convey that message to the people
who would hunt and kill them for nothing more than sport.

Most sharks don't reach sexual maturity until they're about seven years old, and then they only have very small litters. In tournaments, fishermen are often catching juvenile sharks, so not only are the sharks dying, but it's before they have a chance to reproduce and bolster the population.

The industrial fishing industry is responsible for most of the 100 million shark deaths per year, many for nothing but their fins. I came across this big eye thresher shark caught in a net in the Gulf of California in Mexico and felt overwhelming sympathy for the plight of these incredible animals. I hope that through photography I can share my experiences and get people to really care about sharks' lives.

Fins fetch the highest price of all of a shark's body parts.
It was troubling to watch these makos (above) and threshers
(opposite) be dragged onto a beach and broken down for
parts. Often I wish that I could take people who do this out to
the water and show them sharks the way that I see them.

At the Bimini Sharklab, researchers capture and tag nearly every lemon shark born on the island of Bimini in the Bahamas. During pupping season the team sets up gill nets and patrols through the night to record information about each individual shark, and tags them for future identification purposes. After tagging, these young sharks are put in a holding pen like this to ensure that researchers aren't duplicating any data. They are released after a couple days into the wild.

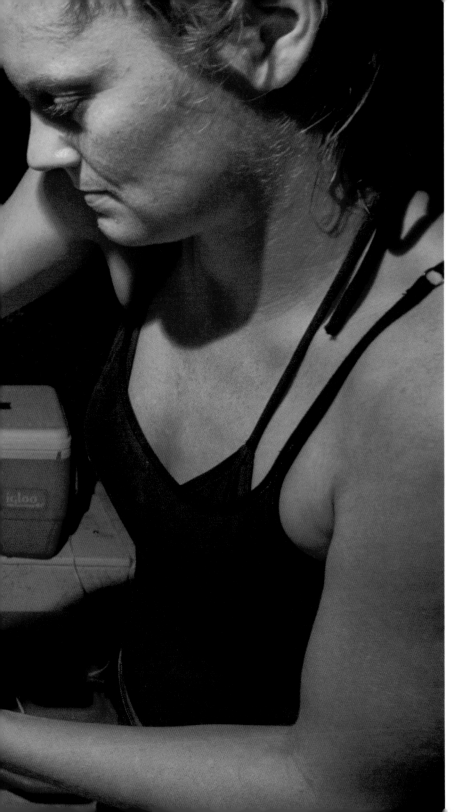

Two researchers from the Bimini Sharklab weigh and measure a baby lemon shark at the Bimini nursery. Their research team is studying why lemon sharks return to the same location to give birth and learning more about how female lemon sharks mate and give birth.

Researchers inject a passive integrated transponder (PIT) tag into a baby lemon shark. These tags act like a bar code for sharks and allow researchers to mark animals without altering their external appearance. When a tagged shark is recaptured, scientists can identify it and keep a log of its growth and travel patterns over the course of its life.

Doc Gruber, head of the Bimini Sharklab, flips a
baby lemon shark over in the water at the edge of
the mangrove nursery. When flipped on their backs,
some species of sharks (including lemons) enter a state
called tonic immobility, a natural state of paralysis.

Wes Pratt attaches a satellite tag to a great hammerhead's enormous dorsal fin. These tags collect geographical data tracking the animal's location, including the depth of water. They stay on the animal for about 90 days before popping off and floating to the surface, providing researchers with valuable information about sharks' migration patterns.

Neil Hammerschlag affixes a National Geographic Critter Cam to a tiger shark in the Bahamas. This tiger left the shallow waters near Tiger Beach for deeper water before returning to the shallows where divers might offer him food. Sharks' lives are full of so much more nuance and wonder than many people realize. They're intelligent animals with rich lives—not just predators to be feared.

Wes Pratt tags an oceanic whitetip shark in the Bahamas. I know not everyone will have the chance to interact with sharks the way I have, so sharing these experiences is the next best thing I can do. Protecting these species protects the ocean, and protects the planet.

There is so much that we still don't know about great white sharks and their lives. As we study them in new habitats, we're piecing together the extent of their intelligence, sociality, and behavior. But threats like overfishing and habitat loss are putting these incredible animals at risk. If we want to continue to learn about this ancient species and the critical role they play in the world's oceans, we need to protect them.

Millennium Atoll, a remote island in the central Pacific, is a reef
shark's paradise. It's one of the world's few remaining coral
ecosystems nearly untouched by humans. The central lagoon
is a shallow, enclosed space filled with blacktip reef sharks,
along with giant clams and small fish and crustaceans.

Blacktip reef sharks—a species that is threatened by commercial fishing operations—use Millennium Atoll's lagoon as a nursery. Young sharks can explore the reef in an area safe from roving predators and fishermen. The island rises only about 20 feet above sea level, and rising waters present a real threat to this crucial shark habitat.

The unusual head shape of the hammerhead—one of the most distinctive species of shark—gives it an impressive field of vision for hunting in the open water. Hammerheads reproduce only once a year, so commercial fishing has a drastic impact on their populations.

At Kingman Reef, a pristine coral reef environment is the backbone of a thriving, diverse population of animals. Sharks may be at the top of the food web, but every part plays an important role in maintaining a healthy and balanced ocean. As the oceans respond to the effects of climate change, it's important that we support and respect every part of the complex ocean environment.

FOLLOWING PAGES: A mako shark swims through the bright, clear waters near San Diego. This is one of my favorite places to photograph sharks, where they freely roam the open waters.